Great Americana

A Treatyse of the Newe India

Sebastian Münster

A Treatyse of the Newe India

by Sebastian Münster
Translated by Rycharde Eden

READEX MICROPRINT

Foreword

A treatyse of the newe India, printed in London in 1553, consists of an English translation of part of the fifth book of Sebastian Münster's *Cosmographiae universalis* of 1550, which reports voyages of Columbus, Vespucci, and Magellan. The German geographer Sebastian Münster excelled in brilliant description, and his massive *Cosmographiae* became the standard European geography for a hundred years. The translator, Richard Eden, had become interested in cosmography at Cambridge and became an ardent advocate of English exploration and colonization.

Eden's *Treatyse* was the second narrative describing the New World to be published in English, and Eden was apparently inspired to print it by the inaccuracy of the earlier anonymous work entitled *Of the newe landes*. Feeling that there was "no lesse inequalitye betwene the tytle and the booke, then if a man woulde professe to wryte of Englande, and entreated onelye of Trumpington, a vyllage wythin a myle of Cambrydge," he decided to provide something better. In his dedication to the Duke of Northumberland he apologized for his own book's incompleteness but solaced himself that "they which set forth or take upon them this viage...may in this smal boke as in a little glasse, see some cleare light ...how to behaue themselues and direct theyr viage to their most commoditie."

The voyages related in Eden's translation mainly concerned Cathay, South America, and the Indies, but mention was made of "Regio Baccalearum [the Newfoundland area]" and "Terra Florida," with the suspicion that they were part of one continent. Eden himself, in his epistle to the reader, made no bones about describing America as the "fourth part of the world," generally at this time considered "three-nooked," as Shakespeare was to put it. No other Englishman had yet stated so flatly in print a fact that many scholars and explorers privately suspected.

Eden's choice of a dedicatee for the *Treatyse* was unfortunate. The book appeared shortly before Northumberland was attainted and executed for his plot to place Lady Jane Grey on the throne. Any hopes Eden may have had of advancing the cause of English exploitation of the New World by Northumberland's influence were thus disappointed. But he had made a start in informing the English reading public of the "good successe and rewarde of noble and honeste enterpryses, by the which not only worldly ryches are obtayned, but also God is glorified, and the Christian fayth enlarged," as he expressed it on the book's title page. Many other voices were to expound this message in print in succeeding decades, until England finally established a firm foothold on the North American continent.

Eden's *Treatyse* and other writings are discussed by Edward Arber, ed., *The First Three English Books on America* (Birmingham, 1885). His contribution to the concept of America as a fourth part of the world is stressed by Franklin T. McCann, *English Discovery of America to 1585* (New York, 1952).

❡ To the right

hyghe and mighty Prince, the
Duke of Northumberlande,
hys grace.

Reade in auncient wrii-
ters (moſt noble prince)
how that mightie kyng
and conquerour of the
world, Alexander the great, at ſuch
tyme as he beheld ẙ tombe of fearſe
Achilles, & therewith called to his
remēbraunce howe excellently the
Poet Homere had ſet forth his he-
roical factes, which notwithſtādīg
he thoughte to be muche inferiour
vnto his, he ſighed & ſayde: Oh the
moſt fortunate, which haſte founde
ſuch a trope to magnifi thi doinges,
meaning hereby, that the fame of A-
chilles was no leſſe notable to hys
poſteritie by homers writing, thē it
was in hys lyfe tyme by hys owne

aa. 4.   martial

martial affayres. Wherby we maye
perceue such magnanimitie to haue
ben in our predicessours, men of noble & stout courage, ẏ they thought
it not sufficiente in their life time to
deserue prayse & honour, except the
same might also redounde to theyr
posteritie, ẏ they mighte therby bee
encouraged to do the like. Whyche
thing truely hath ben ẏ cause, ẏ in al
ages, noble enterprises haue ben cō-
mended, & such as haue attempted
ẏ same, haue bene honoured. Wherfore if honest cōmendacions be a iust
reward dew to noble enterprises, so
much do they robbe & spoyle from ẏ
dignitie therof, which in any poynt
diminishe the same: no lesse confoun-
dinge the order of thinges, then he
whiche cloteth an ape in purple, & a
king in sackecloth. This I speake ẏ
rather, beecause there chaunsed of
late to come to my handes, a shiete
of printed paper, (more worthy so to
be

bee called then a boke) entytuled
of the newe founde landes. The
whyche tytle when I readde, as
one not btterlye ignoraunt hereof.
hauynge before in my tyme readde
Decades, and also the nauigations *de
nouo orbe*, there seemed too me no
lesse inequalitye betwene the tytle
and the booke, then if a man woulde
professe to wryte of Englande, and
entreated onelye of Trumpington
a vyllage wythin a myle of Cam=
brydge. Wherefore partelye mo=
ued the good affeccion, whyche I
haue euer borne to the science of
Cosmographie, whyche entreatsly
of the descripcion of the worlde,
whereof the newe founde landes
are no smal part, & much more by ζ
good wyll, whych of duetie I beare
to my natyue countrey & countrey=
mē, which haue of late to their greāt
prayse (whatsoeuer succede) attēp=
ted ἢ newe viages to serche ζ seas

and newe found landes, I thought it
worthy my trauaple, to their better
comfort, (as one not otherwise able
to further theyr enterprise) to trãs=
late this boke oute of latin into En=
glishe. The which, albeit it do not so
largely or particulerlye entreate of
euery part, region or cõmoditie of ŷ
sayd new found landes, as the wor=
thines of the thing might requyre:
yet sure I am that aswel they which
set forth or take vpõ thẽ this viage,
as also they which shal hereafter at=
tempt ŷ lyke, may in this smal boke
as in a little glasse, see some cleare
light, not only how to learne by the
example dãmage, good successe, and
aduētures of other, how to behaue
them selues & direct theyr viage to
their most cõmoditie, but also if tr̄w
successe herein shoulde not chaunce
according vnto theyr hope & expec=
tatiõ (as oftẽtimes chãceth in great
affaires,) yet not for one foyle or fal,
so to be dismayd as with shame and
                              dishonor

dishonor to leaue wyth losse, but rather to the death to persist in a god-
ly, honeste, & lawful purpose, know-
ing that wheras one death is dewe
to nature, the same is more honourably spēt in such attemptes as may
be to the glorye of God & cōmoditie
of our countrey, then in soft beddes
at home, amōg the teares & weping
of women. Which manlye courage
(like vnto that which hath ben seen
and proued in your grace, aswell in
forene realmes, as also in this oure
countrey) yf it had not been wāting
in other in these our dayes, at suche
time as our souereigne Lord of noble memorie kinge Henry the. viij.
about the same yere of his raygne,
furnished & sent forth certen shippes
vnder the gouernaunce of Sebastian Cabot yet liuing, & one syr Thomas Perte, whose faynt heart was
the cause that that viage toke none
effect, yf (I say) such manly courage

wherof

wherof we haue spoken, had not at that tyme bene wanting, it myghte happelye haue comen to passe, that that riche treasurye called Perularia (which is now in Spayne in the citie of Ciuile, and so named, foz that in it is kepte the infinite ryches bzought thither frō the newe found land of Peru,) myght longe since haue bene in the towze of London, to the kinges great honoure and welth of this his realme. What riches the Emperoure hath gotten oute of all the newe founde landes, it may wel appeare, wheras onlye in the Ilandes of Hispana oz Hispaniola and Cuba & other Ilandes there aboute, were gathered in two monethes twelue thousand poundes weyght of gold as youre grace maye reade in this boke, in the descripcion of the Ilandes. Yet speake I here nothynge of perles, pzecious stones, and spices. Neyther yet of the greate aboun-

daunce

daunce of golde, whiche is engendred almost in al regions neare vnto the *Æquinoctial* line. And wheras I am aduertised ý youre grace haue bene a greate fortherer of thys viage, (as you haue bene euer studious for the commoditie of your countrey,) I thought my trauayl herein coulde no wayes be more worthely bestowed, then to dedicate the same vnto your grace: Most humbly desiringe youre honoure so to accepte mine intente herein, as one whose good will hath not wanted to gratifie your grace with a better thing if mine abilitie were greater. Thus Almighty God preserue your grace in health and honour long to continue.

℟ Your graces poore oratour Rychard Eden.

Of the heare of this serpēt, is made a certayne cloth, which being cast in the fyre when it is foule, is thereby made cleane and very white if it remaine there for ꝑ space of an houre. Suche other innumerable & marueilous thinges, writeth Paulus uenetus that he hath sene and founde in his nauigacions into these partes : of whom also I haue gathered thus muche, lettinge passe manye other thinges whereof he speaketh more at large.

Here endeth the descripció of the Nauigacions from Spayne to the newe India Eastward, & foloweth of the newe Ilandes and India found in the West Ocean sea, from Spayne Westward and Southweste.

⸿ Of the newe

India and Ilādes in the West Ocean sea, how, when, and by whō they were found.

Hristophorus Columbus , A Christe Gentlemē of Italie, *phorus* and borne in the citie *Coliibus.* of *Genua*, when he had been longe conuersaunt in the kyng of Spaynes courte, he applyed hys mynde to searche vnknowen partes of the worlde. And for his better surtheraunce herein, made humble peticion to the kinge, to ayde hym in this his enterpryse, which doubtlesse should redowde to his great honour, and no litle cōmoditie to all the hole countreye of Spayne, yf by his helpe & charges, he might fynde newe regions. But

G. iiij.　　the

the Kinge and Quene laughed him
to scorne, saying: that his ymagina-
cion was but vayne and phantasti-
call. At the length, eyght yeares beynge passed ouer, and Columbus styll
persistinge in his purpose and sute,
the Kyng began to geue eare to his
talke, and after muche reasoninge &
debating of the matter, determined
to trie the witte of the manne. And
there vpō cōmaunded a foyst & two
brigantines to be furnished with all
kynde of ordinaunce and bitayles:
which being prepared, the fyrst day
of September, in the yere of Christ
1492, Columbus departed from the
coastes of Spayne, and wente for-
warde in his biage longe desyred.
And when he had passed the Ilādes
called Gades, he diuerted toward the
fortunate Ilandes called Insule Fortunate, which are now called Canarie, because they are full of dogges. They
were in time past called Fortunate,
for

Great
enterpri-
ses haue
euer ben
coūnted
phātasti
call.

the fyrst
biage of
Christo-
phorus
Colūbus.

the Ilan-
des cal-
led Ga-
des.

The Ilā-
des of
Canaria

for the excellente temperatenes of the ayre, and greate fruytefulnes. *Columbus* departinge from hense, sayled towarde the Weste, and at the length founde certayne Ilandes, of the whiche two were very greate, wherof the one he called Hispana, and the other Iohanna.

¶ Of the two Ilandes Iohanna and Hispana.

AS *Columbus* came to the Ilande whiche he called Iohanna, he Iohanna hearde a merueylous sweete noyse of innumerable byrdes, and especiallye of Nightingales whiche wandred in the thicke wooddes in the Moneth of Nouembre. He founde also mooste fayre Ryuers, swete to drinke, & many goodly hauēs. And as he sayled by the costes of the Ilande Southwestewarde,
and

and could fynd no ende, he thought
it had been the mayne land, & ther=
fore determyned to drawe backe,
being partly enforsed by roughnes
of the sea: and thus returning some
what Eastward, he came to an Ilãd
Hispana,
or: Hispa
niola.
whiche he afterwarde called Hispana,
where arriuing to the land, he & his
companye was sene of the Inhabi=
tantes of the Iland, which sodeinly
fled into the thicke woodes: whom
the Spanyardes pursewinge, toke
a womanne whom they brought to
theyr shippe, entreatinge her verye
gentillye, fyllinge her with delicate
meates and wyne, and clothing her
in fayre apparel, & so let her depart:
for thei goe naked, and are not vsed
to delicates. And as this womanne
returned to her companie, some be=
ynge moued by the lyberalitie de=
clared vnto her, came by greate
multitudes to the sea bankes, brin=
ginge golde with them, which they
chaunged

chaunged for earthen pottes, and drinkinge glasses. Thus a further frendſhip by this meanes contracted, the Spanyardes begonne more diligētly to ſearche theyr maner of lyuinge and maners, ᶇ ſo vnderſtode that they had a king. And therefore entering further into the Iland, they were honorably receyued of the king. Thei vewyde their houſes, and merueyled to ſee them ſo bylded without the vſe of Iron, which they are vtterly without: in the ſtede wherof they vſe a certeyn ſtone, wherwith they cut and ſawe theyr timbre.

gold for earth ᶇ glaſſe.

the king of the Iſland.

Bylding without the vſe of Iron.

¶ Of the people called *Canibales* or *Anthropophagi*, which are accuſtomed to eate mans fleſhe.

Wheras the people of the forenamed Iſlādes, fled at the ſight of our menne, the cauſe thereof was, that they ſuſpected them to haue

haue been *Canibals*, that cruel & fearſe people which eate mãs fleſhe, which nacion our men had ouerpaſſed, leaninge them on the ſouthſyde. But after they had knowledge of the cõtrary, they made greuous cõplaynt to our men, of the beaſtly and fearſe

maners of theſe *Canibales*, which were no leſſe cruel agaynſt them, thẽ the Tyger oꝛ the Lyon agaynſte tame beaſtes. Declaring furthermoꝛe, ẏ when ſoeuer they take any of them vnder the age of .xiiij. yeares, they vſe to gelde them, & francke thẽ vntyll they be very fat, as we are wõt to doe with capons oꝛ hennes: and as foꝛ ſuche as dꝛawe towarde .xx. yeare olde, to kyll them foꝛthwith and pull out theyꝛ guttes, and eate the ſame freſhe and newe, wyth o-

ther extreme partes of the bodye, poudering the reſidue with ſalte, oꝛ keping it in a certayne pickle as we do iegottes oꝛ ſanſages. Yet eate they

they not the womē, but reserue thē to encrease, as we doe hennes to lay egges. And if thei take any old womē, they kepe thē for dzudges. And therfore whē the Canibales make incursion, the people of these Ilādes flye with all spede. For albeit they vse arrowes, yet are they not able to resyste theyr fearsenes.

⸿Of the maners of the inhabitantes of the Iland of Hispana and of suche thynges as are found there.

The inhabitātes of this Ilande, vse in ý stede of bzead, certayne rotes like vnto nauie rotes, hauing the tast of soft & grene chestnuttes. Gold wt thē is in estimaciō, for they hāge certayne peces therof at their eares: they go not out of ý limities yf their own cōtrie, nor exercise any marchādise wt strāgers: thei gather gold in ý sādes of a certē riuer which spzingeth out of veri high mōtaines

Rootes in ý stede of bread

Gold is estimaciōn.

Golde golde is gathred.

They

They gather it with great laboure
and melte it and caste it, fyrste into
masses or wedges, and afterwarde
into brode plates . They haue no
foure foted beastes, except connies:
they haue serpentes of monstrous
greatnes, but without hurte or venime . They haue also wylde turtle
doues & duckes, muche greater then
ours, & gese whyter then swannes,
sauing ý they haue redde heades.
Thei haue also many popingiayes:
some grene, some yelowe, and some
not muche vnlyke them of India,
w redde circles about their neckes
This Iland bringeth forth also Ma-
stix, Aloe, and suche other gumes :and
especially certayne redde graynes,
which are sharper then pepper.

Serpēts wythout venime.

Popin-giapes.

Spices & Gumes

¶How Columbus, after he had
found new Ilādes, returned
agayne to Spayne, where
preparinge a newe nauie, he
toke his viage to ý Canibales.
Columbus,

Columbus, not a little ioyeful of the Ilandes newly found, the spring tyme drawing nere, he determined to returne to his countrey: leauing with the king of the Iland. 38. men which should diligently searche the situacion of the Ilande, the maners of the people, & the natures of trées and fruites. But he, loyseninge vp his sayles, directed hys viage towarde Spayne, bringing with him tenne menne of the sayd Ilande, to thende that they mighte learne the Spanishe tonge, which they might easely doe, because al the wordes of theyr language may well be writtē with our letters. Columbus, after thys his returne, and fortunate successe in his fyrste viage, was honorablye receyued of the Kynge and Quene, and greatlye magnified with innumerable glorious tittles: willinge that he should no more thenceforth be called Columbus, but the Admiral of the

The Indian tōg

Columbus, at his returne, is made Admiral of the Ocean sea.

the great Ocean sea: and prepared for him towarde his second viage. xvij. foistes and. xij. brigstines, wel furnished with al kynd of artillerye and plentie of vitayles, and in them twelue hundreth men wel appoynted: Corne also to sowe, & al kindes of seedes and plantes. For, excepte pine apple trees & date trees, there growe none in these Ilandes that are knowen to vs. The Admirall toke also with him al sortes of Iron tooles to thintent to byld townes & fortresses where his men might lye in safegarde. Therfore the first day of September departing from the Ilandes called Gades, with a prosperous wind he arryued at the Iland of Canaria the fyrst daye of October: from whense directing his viage towarde the lefte hande, he sayled toward ye South, & at ye length came to the Ilades of the Canibals. And because he came thether on the Sun-

days

called the Dominical day, he called the Iland
the Iland where he arryued, Dominica: of Domi
which when he perceyued to be but nicas
saluage and rude, he sayled on further: and in twentie dayes sayling,
came to another Iland replenished
with al kindes of trees, frō which came _Insula_
a marueylous fragrant sauour: By _Crucis._
reason whereof, some being allured
by the pleasantnes of the place, wēt
aland, where they sawe no kynde of
lyuinge beastes, sauinge lysertes of _Lisertes_
wonderful houdge greatnes. This
Ilande he called _Insula Crucis_, whiche
was also an Ilande of the _Canibales,_ as
afterward they proued in dede. For
as they sayled about the Ilād, they Houses
found certayne lowe cotages made of trees.
of trees, lyke vnto stagies. For they
set trees vpright in order round a-
bout, fasteninge postes in them crosse
ouer, where vnto the trees cleaue
faste, so that by this meanes they cā
not fall. They frame the rooses of

H.i.   thes

these cotages, with sharpe toppes
after the maner of rownde tentes.
And last of al, they inclose and couer
these trees thus set in ozder, wyth
the leaues of date trees, and certen
other trees, to thintent to make thē
a stronger defence agaynst wynd ⁊
wether. And within the cotage,
they tye the postes together with
ropes of bombage cotton, and a certayne longe roote. They haue cou-
ches made, one aboue another, the
flowzes whereof they strawe wyth
heye and cotton. And as soone as
they hadde spied our men, they fled
incontinente. And when oure men
came into theyz houses, they found

Younge
men stal
le i to be
made
fatte.

in them certayne young men bound
to postes, and kept to be made fatte,
and lykewyse many olde womenne
which these Canibales kepte to be their

Fine co-
kerye.

dzudges. They founde there also
earthen vesselles of all sortes, in
which they sodde mens flesshe with
popin-

popingiayes, greese, & duckes flesshe, al together in one vessell. They rosted also mans flesshe vpon spyttes, reseruing the bones of the armes & legges, whiche they vse in the stede of Jron, to piece & typpe theyr arrowes. For they are vtterlye without Jron. The found also the head of a yong mã, yet bleding and fastened to a poste. But certayne woamenne whiche had stedde from the Canibales to oure menne, the Jdmiral commaunded to be gorgiously decked after the maner of our women, and with many rewardes to be sent agayne to theyr owne companye. By meanes whereof, the Canibales beynge allured by the lyberalitie and gyftes of our men, hoping that they also shoulde be lykewyse rewarded, came running toward our men: but whẽ they drew somwhat nere vnto them, they fled immediatly into the nexte wooddes. And thus oure men

Canibales allured with lyberalitie

H. ij.   departing

departing from thence, returned to the Ilande of Hispana.

CHow the Admirall passed manye Ilandes, and what thynges chaunced to hym & his companie in that viage.

AS the Admirall departed frō the Iland of the Canibales, & wēt foreward on his viage, he passed by many Ilandes: among the whiche was one called Matinina, in whyche dwell only women, after the maner of thē, called Amazones, as he learned of the men of the Ilandes which he brought with him into Spayne at his fyrste viage, and saued them frō the fearsenes of the Canibales. He passed also innumerable other Ilādes, of which to some he gaue names, as Mons Parratus, Sancta Maria rotunda, Sancta Martinus, Sancta Maria antiqua, and Sancta Crux, Into the which oure men entering to thintente to fetche fresshe water, found foure Canibales, which had takē foure

Matinina an Ilād of wōmē onelye.

The names of sundrye Ilandes

foure yonge women: who, as soone
as thei had spied our men, wringed
theyr handes, seming therby to de=
syre ayde of oure men : at whose co=
ming to delyuer them, the men fled
into the woodes and lest the womē.
Shortly after , our men saw a bote
coming on the sea with. viij. mē and
as many women: with whom oure
men bickeringe lost one of theyr cō=
panions , by reason that these bar=
bariens are accustomed to infecte
theyr arrowes w benime: yet oure
men preuayled and slewe parte of
them , and broughte the resydue by
forse to the Admyrall. As they de=
parted from hence , they found ma=
ny other Ilandes, but such as they
could not come to for the roughnes
of the sea and multitude of rockes.
But some of the smallest brigatines
which drewe no great depth, went
somewhat nearer, and noumbred a=
boue seuen and fortie Ilandes , and
　　　　H.iij.　　　　called

arrowes
infected
w beni=
me.

called the place Archipelagus. Sayling
from hence, they found another I-
land called Buchema, into the whiche ⅌
Canibales make sundry incursions, by
reason whereof the inhabitantes are
at continual warre with thē. Thus
at the length, the Admiral with his
hole naute returned to the Iland of
Hispania: but in an euyl tyme. For they
whiche he hadde lefte there for a
garrison, were all dead: as were also they whiche he toke with him frō
the same Ilande into Spayne to
vse them for intrepretours . Of
whiche seuen dyed by chaunge of
the ayre . One of them was permitted of the Admirall to departe,
when the naute came neare to hys
countrey. The residue stole awaye
priuelye, and swamme to lande: but
the Admirall doubting whether all
his men were dead or no, whiche he
left in the Iland, commaunded certayne ordinaunce to be shot of, that
by the

by the noyſe thereof they myghte
haue warning to come forth, yf any
tarye lurkinge in corners : but none
appeared, whoſe fartall dayes had
fyniſhed theyr lyfe . At the length,
the kyng of the Ilande beyng ther=
to enforſed, declared the hole mat=
ter to the Admyrall as well as he
coulde by interpretours : affyrming
that there were in the Iland other
Kinges beſyde him : and of greater
power then he, which were ſore of=
fended that the Spaniardes hadde
ſubdued the Ilandes : ȝ in reuenge
therof, came to the town where the
Spaniardes lay, which they ouer=
came ȝ burnt, ȝ ſlew al the mē ther=
in : and that he alſo at the ſame con=
flicte, taking part with our mē, was
ſore woūded with an arrow on the
arme, for the better tryall where=
of he bore hys arme in a towell,
becauſe it was not yet hole of that
wounde . But ſhortelye after
H. iiij. they

the kiag
diſſem
bleth w
the Ad=
myrall

they had knowledge, that the king fayned this tale: so that he hardely escaped the handes of the Admiral, who was determyned wyth some kynd of punishment to haue examined him further. But he suspecting the matter, fled into the inner partes of the Iland, declaring therby, that he was the destruction of our men: who, certayn of our companie, pursuinge, founde manye marueylous thinges: and especiallye ryuers in which is founde muche golde, and a mountayne, whose sande is sparkeled with gold. In this place, the Admiral bylded a citie, which he compassed about with a walle. And departing from hence, he searched almost all the Iland: in the inner partes wherof he bylded a towre, & named it, S. Thomas towre, whiche he made to thintent that he might the more safely searche out the secretes of so plentifull a region, and especially the

Golde founde in riuers & mountaines

ally the gold mines of the same: and thus leauinge a garrison there, he departed, takinge with him three foystes, wherwith he sayled to seke newe Ilandes, and came first to the Ilande of Cuba, and from thence to Iamiaca, being greater then Sicilia, very fruytful and wel inhabited. Which, whē he had vewed, he departed frō thence, & sayled about the sea costes where he sawe innumerable other small Ilandes, standinge so thicke, that the ship was in maner borne a lande: and was therfore enforsed to returne home, the same way which he came.

℄How the Spaniardes abused the submissiō & frendeshippe of the inhabitantes of the Ilandes.

IN this meane tyme, the Spaniardes which the admiral had left in the Iland of Hispana, had euyll entreated the inhabitauntes: so that

for

for wante of bitayles & foode, they
begonne to famyne : imputinge the
fault hereof vnto the Chꝛiſtian mē,
The cru
eltie of
the Chꝛi
ſtian mē
which had digged vp al the ꝛootes
wherwith thei were accuſtomed to
make theyꝛ bꝛead . And whereas
they yet perceaued, that ẏ Chꝛiſtien
men entended to cōtinue there, thei
ſent an ambaſſadour to the admiral
to deſyꝛe him to reſtrayne the out-
ragiouſnes and crueltie of his men,
at whoſe hādes they ſuſtained ſuch
iniuries and biolēce, as they ſcarce-
ly loked foꝛ at the handes of moꝛtal
enemies. Declaringe further , that
vnder the pꝛetēce of ſeking foꝛ golð
they cōmitted innumerable wꝛōges
Crueltie
of coue-
touſnes.
and miſchieuous actes , ſpoyl'ng in
maner all the hole region : and that
foꝛ the auoꝛding of ſuch enoꝛmities
and oppꝛeſſions, they hadde rather
paye tribute , then to be thus dayly
vexed with incurſiōs, & neuer to be
at quiete. Upon this complaynte it
was

was agreed, that they shoulde paye
yearely tribute to the Christian king
& that they should applie the selues
to gather and encrease theyr rotes,
whiche were to them in the stede of
flowre and wheat: and so consumed
that with great labour they coulde
scarcely fynde any in the wooddes.
They payde therefore for their tribute, euery thre monethes, certayn
pound weyghtes of gold: but suche
as had no gold, payde spyces, & gossampine cotton. In the meane time
the Spaniardes, who should haue
been occupied in digging for golde,
gaue the selues to play, wantónes &
idlenes, cótemning, & falling into ha
tered wt their gouernour, by which
theyr liceciousnes, the people of the
Iland beyng prouoked, became more
disobedient & wyld, degeneratinge
fró al kind of honestie & faithfulnes:
yea ý spaniardes also became so neg
ligét in sekíng for gold, ý sometyme
the

Bread of
rotes.

The tri-
bute of
the bar-
barians

Disobe-
dience tur
neweth
idlenes

the charges exceaded the gaynes.
Neuerthelesse in the yere of Christ,
1501.they gathered within ý space

of two monethes twelue thousand

poundes weyght of golde. But the
Admirall appoyntinge his brother
Bartholomeus Columbus, to be gouernour
of the Iland, he in the yeare.1495.
determined to returne to Spayne,
to certifye the kyng of al these mat-
ters. In which viage, he manfullye
defended him self in battayl againft
the rebelles of certayne other I-
landes which had cõspyred agaynst
the Spanyardes.

¶How the Portugals sought
new Ilādes in the East partes,
and how they came to Calicut.

IN this meane tyme that ý Spanyardes soughte newe and vnknowen landes in the West partes,
the Portugales attempted to doe
the same in the Easte partes . And
least one of them should be a lette or
hinderaunce

Bartholo-
meus
Coũbus,

hinderaunce to the other, they deuyded the world betwene them by the
aucthoritie of the Bishop of Rome,
Alexāder the. vi. of that name. And
that on this condicion, that frō the
Ilandes called *Hesperides* (whiche are
now called *caput ueride*) the one shoulde
saple Westwarde, and the other towarde the South pole, thus deuy-
ding the world betwene thē in two
equal partes. So that whatsoeuer
vnknowen landes shoulde be discouered in the Easte partes, the same
to be dewe to the Portugales: And
all suche as shoulde be founde in the
Weste partes, to appertayne to the
Spanyardes. Whereby it came to
passe, that the Spaniardes, euer by
the South, sayled into the Weste,
where they founde a large mayne
lād, with Ilādes great ⁊ litle innumerable, hauing in them great plē-
tie of golde and pearles, and other
great riches. But the Portugales,
by

The bi-
shop of
rome de-
uideth ȳ
world.

hesperi-
des, or Ca-
put ueri-
de.

How the
Spany-
ardes ⁊
ȳ Portu-
gales de-
uideth the
world be-
twene
them.

Golde ⁊
Pearles

The Equinoctial lyne.

The ryuer of Ganges

Calicut.

Taprobana

Samotra.

the great cytie of malaccha

the regiõ of sinaru

the Ilandes of Molucca

by the Southe, and costes of the Jlandes called Hesperides, and Equinoctial lyne, ⁊ Tropicus Capricorni, came ŷ into East, by the goulfe called sinus Persicus, euen vnto the costes of India, within the riuer of Ganges; wheras is now the great market towne, ⁊ kingedõ of Calicut. And frõ thence to the Jlãd of Taprobana, (now called Sumetra, Zamara or Samotra) ⁊ so forth to Aures Chersonesus, wheras is nowe the great cytie of Malaccha, beyng one of ŷ most famous market townes of al ŷ East partes. From Malaccha, they entered into a great goulfe, by which they came to the region of sinarum. Not farre from Malaccha, are the Jlandes called Molucca, in which al kyndes of spyces growe and are brought to the cytie of Malaccha. But the Spanyardes hauing knowledge what greate cõmoditie the Portugales had receyued by the Jlandes of Molucca, attempted

ted to proue yf they also might find
the same Ilandes in sayling so farre
Westward, that the y mighte at the
length by West and southwest come
into the East, as by good reaso they
presupposed the roundnesse of the
earth would permitte, if they were
not otherwyse lette by the fyrme or
mayne land lyinge in the waye and
stoppinge theyr passage, whereof as
yet was no certeyntie knowe. And
this dydde they to thintent that by
this meanes they myghte more ea-
selye and wyth lesse charge bringe
spyces from thence into Spayne.
Therefore, the maner of this viage
was, that they shoulde sayle from
the Weste, vnder the lowest hemis-
pherye or halfe copasse of the earth,
& so to come into the East. A thinge
surelye that myghte seeme verye
harde to attempte, beecause it was
vncertayn

Sayling
into the
East by
the west
the rond-
nes of
ye erth.
The fir-
me land

Spices
the bringe
from the
West in
to the
Easte.

vncertaine whether that, most pru-
dente and beneficiall nature , (who
worketh al thinges with most high
prouidence) had not so deuided and
seperated the East from the West,
partely by sea, and partely by land,
that there might by this way haue
been no passage into the East. For it
was not yet knowen, whether that

America.
great region of America, (whiche they

The firs
me land.
call the fyrme or mayne lande) dyd
seperate the Weste sea fro the East:
But it was founde that that fyrme
lande exteded from the West to the
South: And that also towarde the

Regio
Baccalea
rum.
Terra
Florida.
North partes were foud two other
regios, whereof the one is called Regio Baccalearum, & the other Terra Florida:
which, if they were adherent to the
sayde fyrme land , there could be no
passage by the Weste seas into the
East India, forasmuch as ther was
not yet founde any strayghte of the
sea, wherby any enteraunce mighte
be

be ope into the East. In this meane
while, the kyng of Spayne beynge
elected Emperoure, prepared a na
uie of fyue shippes, ouer the whiche
he appointed one Magellanus to be cap
tayne, commaundinge him that he
should sayle towarde the coastes of
the sayd fyrme land, dyrectinge his
viage by the south partes thereof,
vntyl he had eyther found the ende
of the same, or elles some streyghte
wherby he mighte passe to those o=
doriferous Ilandes of Molucca, so fa=
mously spoken of for the great abu=
daunce of swete sauours and spices
founde therein. The shippes there=
fore, beyng well furnished with all
thinges necessarie, Magellanus depar=
tinge from Ciuile in Spayne, the
tenth day of August, in the yeare of
Christ. 1519. came fyrst to ye Ilades
of Canaria, and from thence to the I=
landes called Hesperides: from whiche
dyrectinge hys course betwene the

J.i. Weste

the kitg
of spayn
sendeth
foorth
shippes

The via
ge of Ma
gellanus,
by the
west in=
to ye east.

The Ila
des of
Molucca.

The Ila
des of Ca
naria.

West and the East toward the sayd fyrme land, in few dayes with prosperous sayling, he discouered a corner or poynt of the sayd mayne lád, called Promontorium Mariæ, where the people dwell, called Canibales, whiche are accustomed to eate mans fleshe. Fró hence he sayled on southwarde by the long tracte of this firme lád, which reacheth so farre into ý south and extendeth so many degrees beyond ý circle called Tropicus Capricorni, ý the south pole (called pole Antartike) is there eleuated fortie & fyue degrees. And thus beyng brought into the East, they saw certayn Indians gatheringe shel fysshes by the sea bankes: beyng men of very high stature, clothed ẃ beastes skinnes. To whom, wheras certayne of the Spaniardes went a land, & shewed them belles & paynted papers, they begon to daunce & leape aboute the Spaniardes, with a rude and murmuring songe. At the length there

Promontorium ſ Mariæ.

Canibales

The eleuació of the south pole. 45 degrees

The Region of giauntes,

came three other, as thoughe they were ambassadours, whiche by certayn signes desyred ye Spaniardes to go with thē further into the lād, making a count enaunce as though thei wold intertayn thē wel, where vpō, ye captayne Magellanus sent wt thē vii. mē well instructed, to thintēt to searche ye regiō & maners of the people. And thus they went wt thē into ye desertes, wher they came to a low cotage couered with wylde beastes skinnes, hauing in it two māsiōs, in one of ye which were womē & childrē & in the other only mē. They interteined their gestes after a barbaros & beastly maner, which neuertheles semed to thē princelike: for they killed a beast, not much vnlike a wylde asse, whose flesshe (but halfe rosted) they set before our mē, without any other kind of meate or drinke. Here were our mē of necessitie cōstrained to lye al night vnder these skinnes,

Cotages couered wt beastes skinnes.

Onagre

F.ij.   by

by reason of the great abundaunce
of snowe and wynde. And when it
was day,our mē were very earnest
with them, & would in maner haue
enforsed them to goe with them to
the shippe:whych thing thei perceauing,couered them selues from the
head to the foote with certayn horrible beastes skinnes , and paynted
theyr faces with sundrye colours.
Thus taking theyr bowes and arrowes, & bringing with them other
of theyr companie, of much greater
stature and terrible aspect,thē they
were , they shewed them selues to
oure men in araye,as thoughe they
were ready to fight.But the Spanyardes,whiche thoughte that the
matter would haue comen to hand
strokes, commaunded a piece of ordinaunce to be shotte of.The which
although it dyd no hurte, yet these
hardy giauntes,which a litle before
semed to be as bold as though they
                                    durst

durſt haue made warre againſt Ju-
piter, were by the noyſe therecf put
in ſuche feare, that they foorthwith
beganne to entreate of peace. Our
men entēded to haue brought ſome
of theſe Gyauntes wyth them into
Spayne for the ſtraungenes of the
thinge : but they all eſcaped oute of
theyr handes. ᴹᵃᵍᵉˡˡᵃⁿᵘˢ therfore vn-
derſtandinge that it were vnprofy-
table to tarie there any longer, and
that alſo the ſea was very rough , &
the wether ſtormie and boyſteous,
and that furthermore the firme lād
extēded further toward the ſouth,
in ſo muche , that the ſurther they
ſayled that waye, they ſhould fynde
it ſo much y̆ colder, he deferred hys
proceding vnto the moneth of may,
at whiche time, y̆ ſharpenes of winter, exceadeth with them, whenas
with vs, ſommer is begon. He foūd
there greate plentie of wood . The
ſea alſo miniſtred vnto them great

exɽeme
winter
in maye

abundaunce of shelfishe, besyde other fysshes of sundrie kyndes. He found lykewyse many sprynges of freshe & holesome waters: and vsed huntinge and taking of foules. Only bread & wyne, was lackinge in the shippe.

the south pole ele-uate. xl. degrees

The south pole was there eleuated fortie degrees.

¶ How Magellanus by a strayght or narrow arme of the sea, say-led by the west into the East to dyuers Ilandes : where also he was slayne.

The wynter now beinge past, the xxiiij.day of Auguste , Magellanus departed fro the place aforesayde, & styll solowed the tracte of the firme land toward the south, vntyl at the length, the.xxvi.day of Nouember, he found in that firme land, certayn

The strayght of Magel- lanus.

open places lyke vnto strayghtes or narrow seas. Into the which en-tring with his nauie, he comaunded that certayn shippes should searche the

the goulfes on euerye fyde, yf anye
way oz paſſage might be found into
the Eaſt. At the length, they found a
certayn depe ſtraight, by the which
they were perſwaded ẏ there was
enteraunce into ſome other mayne
ſea, inſo much that *Magellanus* attemp=
ted to ſearche ẏ ſame. This ſtraight
was found to be ſomtime of ẏ bzedth
of thze Italian myles, ſometyme of
two, ⁊ ſometime of tenne, ⁊ reached
ſomwhat toward the Weſt. The al=
titude oz eleuacion of the ſouth pole
in this place, was foúde to be. lii. de=
grees . They coulde ſee no people

The alti
tude of
the ſouth
pole. lii.
degrees.

ſtering in the coſtes of this entraúce
Therfoze *Magellanus* ſeing thys lande
to be rough ⁊ ſaluage, ⁊ vnpleaſaút
to abide in, by reaſo of extreme cold,
he thought it not wozthye the tra=
uayle, to ſpend any time in ſerching
the ſame. Therfoze ſailing fozward
in his viage thus attépted by ẏ ſaid
ſtrayghte, (which is now called the

ſtrayght

strayght of Magellanus) he was therby
brought into another mayn sea, verye great and large . The length of
this strayght oz narrow sea, is este-
med to be a hūdzeth spanishe miles.
The land which he had on his right
hande, he doubted not to be mayne
lande : and that on the left hand, he
supposed to bee Ilandes . Magellanus
sawe lykewyse the fyrme land to be
extended directly toward ÿ Nozth:
wherefoze letting passe that greate
lande , he sayled by that greate and
large sea betwene the West and the
Nozth: ƒ that foz this intente, that
at the length he might by the West
come into the East, and agayne vnder the burning lyne called Zona Torrida, beynge well assured that the I-
landes of Molucca (which he soughte)
were in the Easte, and not farre frō
the Equinoctial lyne. When they hadde
thus sayled fortie dayes , and came
now agayne vnder the liue oz circle
called

called Tropicus Capricorni, they founde two lyttle Jlandes inhabyted, but very barren, and therfore called the infortunate Jlandes. Departinge fro thence, they sailed on for a great space, and found a certayne Jlande which ý inhabitantes called Inuagana, where the eleuacion of the Northe pole, (called pole Artike) was. xj. degrees: And the length from the Jlandes called Gades, by the Weste, was iudged to bee c.lviii.degrees. Thus proceding, they saw dyuers other Jlandes, and that so manye, that they supposed they had been brought into a great sea lyke vnto that called Archipelagus, where with sygnes ⁊ poyntinges (as the dumme are wont to speake with the dumme) they asked of these Jndians, the names of the Jlandes, wherby they learned that thei were in Acatan, and not farre fro the Jlande called Selani, wel inhabited and replenished with

abundaunce

Tropicus capricorns.

the Jlād of Inua gana.

The Jlā des of Gades cal led Cables Males.

Archipe lagus.

Acatan. Selani.

abundaunce of al thinges necessarie for the cōmodities of this life. Saylling therfore toward the Ilande of Selani, thei were with a cōtrary wind drieuen on the Iland of Massana, from whense they came to the greate Island af Subuth, where y̆ Spanyardes were wel enterteyned of the kinge of the Iland, who brought thē into a certayn cotage, and set before thē such delicates as he hadde. Theyr bread, was of the trunke of a certen tree, cut in pieces, & fried with oyle. Theyr drinke was of the humoure or ioyse which droppeth out of the braunches of the date trees, when they are cutte. Theyr meate was suche as they toke by foulinge, with such fruites as the contrei brought forth. This Ilande was very riche of gold and ginger. In these partes Magellanus made warre agaynste the inhabitauntes of certayne other Islandes: In which conflicte, the spaniardes

Massana.

Subuth

Bread of the trūke of trees.

Drinke of the droppīg of date trees.

Golde & Ginger

niardes hauing the ouerthzow Magellanus was slayne with seuen of hys men. When the Spaniardes hadde thus lost theyz captayne, they elected a new gouernoure of theyz nauie, appointing one Iohannes Serranus to that office. Magallanus had also a bond man bozne in the Ilandes of Molucca, whom he had bought in the citie of Malaccha. This bondman vnderstode the Spanisshe tonge: and where as the captayn Serranus could do nothing without him, who now lay sicke by reason of the woūdes which he had receaued in the said conflicte, so that he was fayne to speake sharpely to him and thzeaten to beate him oz he could geat him out of the shyppe, he here vpon conceaued so great hatered and indignacion agaynste the Spanyardes, that he wente immediatlye to the Kinge of Subuth, declaring the couetousnes of the Spaniardes to be vnsaciable, as thei wold

shortely

Mr. Magellanus is slayne.

the new captaiue Serranus is betraied of his boudmā

the king of Subuth cōspyreth agaynst the Spanyardes

shortely vse crueltie against him also, and bring him into subiectiō and seruitude. The barbarous king beleued his wordes, ꝑ therwith pryuelye with the ayde of the other Jlandes, conspired against the Spanyardes, and toke or slew as many of them as came to a banket whereunto they were bidden vnder pretence of frendship. Amōg the which also, Serranus the Captaine was taken prisoner. But the resydue of the Spanyardes which remayned in the shippes, beyng taught ꝑ warned by the euyll chaunce which befell to theyr cōpanions, and fearing greater deceytes and conspiracies, lyft vp their ankers and gaue wind to their sayles. In the meane tyme was Serranus brought bound to the sea bankes, desiring his companions to delyuer or redeme him frō that horrible captiuitie of hys enemies. But the Spaniardes, albeit they

The cap
tayne
Serra-
nus is
takē pri-
soner.

they toke it for a diſhonour, to leaue
or forſake their Captayne, yet fearing fraude or further diſſimulatiō,
they ſayled aſyde from that Iland,
and came to the Ilandes of _Gibeth_ &
Porne. In this mayne ſea, were two
great Ilandes, wherof the one was
called _Siloli,_ & the other _Porne_ the leſſe,
where our mē were wel entreated.
The inhabitantes of _Porne_ honoure
the ſunne and the mone: they keepe
alſo a certayn ciuile iuſtice & ſtēdiy
loue one to another. And aboue all
thinges, deſyre peace and ydlenes.
Therfore their chiefe ſtudie is, in no
caſe to moleſte their neyghboures or
ſtraungers, or to be iniurious to a-
nye man. They haue lyttle houſes,
made of earth and wood, and couered partely with rubbiſhe, & partly
with ẙ bowes of date trees. They
take as manye wyues as they are
able to kepe. Their comon meat, is
ſuch as they take by ſoulinge or fiſ-
ſhing,

The Ilā-
des of
Gibeth &
Porne.

Siloli.

Peace &
Idlenes.

shinge. They make bread of ryce: ⁊ drinke, of the liquour whiche droppeth frō the braunches of date trees, cutte. Some vse marchaundyse in the Ilandes nere about thenr: some applie thē selues to huntinge ⁊ fysshing, and some to husbādry. Theyr apparell, is of Gossampine cotton. They haue greate abundaunce of camphyre, ginger and cinomome.

¶How the Spaniardes came to the Ilandes of *Molucca*, and of the people with great hanging eares.

THe Spaniardes takinge theyr leaue of the king of *Porne*, departed: dyrecting theyr viage towarde the Ilandes of *Molucca*, whiche were shewed vnto thē by the same king. They came fyrst to the costes of the Ilande called *Solo*, where are found Pearles as bygge as turtle doues egges: but they are gathered in the depth of the sea. The inhabitantes

of

of this Ilande, at suche tyme as the
Spanyardes came thether, toke a
shelfyshe of suche houdge bignes, ý
the flesshe therof wayed. xlvij. poūd
weyght. Wherby it is apparaunt ý
great pearles should be found there
forasmuch as pearles are the byrth
of certayn shelfishes. Frō hence thei
came to the Iland of Gilona, in which
are certayn people hauing hanging
eares of such length, that they hang
downe to theyr shoulders. Wherat
as the Spaniardes marueyled, the
men of the Iland tolde thē, that not
farre frō thence was another Ilād
in which were a kind of mē, not onely with hāging eares, but also with
eares of suche breadth and length,
that with one of them they myghte
couer theyr hole head . But the
Spanyardes , who soughte for
golde and spyces , and not for mon-
sters, sayled dyrectly to the Ilādes
of Molucca , where they arryued,
the

A marue-
lous big
shelfishe

Gilona.

Men w
hanging
eares.

The spa
nyardes
arriue at
the Ilan
des of
Molucca.

the eyghte moneth after the death of their gouernour Magellanus. These Ilandes are fyue in noumbre, the names wherof are these. Tharant, Muthil, Thedori, Mare, and Mathien. Some of them are sytuate on thys syde the Equinoctiall lyne, some vnder it, & some beyonde it.   Some beare cloues, some Nutmegges, and some Cinomome. They are not farre distaunt the one from the other . They are but little and narowe. The inhabitantes are very poore, because ther is no encrease of anye other thinge sauing onely of spyces . They lyue with bread and fyshe, and sometime popingiayes . They lurke in lowe cotages: And in fyne, all thinges w them are despicable and vile, beside peace, idlenes, and spices. In Thedori is great plentie of cloues, as also in

The tree that beareth cloues.

Tarante and Mathien. The trees which bringe forth cloues, growe not, but on rockes and broken cliffes, where
some

sometime they grow so thicke, that
they appeare lyke a lyttle wood or
groue. This tree, bothe in leaues,
biggenes, and heyght, is much lyke
vnto the baye tree. It beareth the
fruite in ꝑ toppes of euery brauche.
The budde springeth out fyrst, and
then in it the floure, not much vnlike
the floure of an orange tree. The
cloue is fyrst redde: but after beyng
scorched by the heate of the sonne, it
is made blacke. The inhabitauntes
deuide the groues of these trees betwene them, as we doe the vynes.
The Iland of Muthil, bringeth forth
cino:nome. This tree, is ful of small the cino-
braunches ꝛ baren, beste lyking in a mome
drye soyle, and is very like vnto the tree.
tree, that beareth the pomgranate.
The barke of this tree, by reason of
the great heate of the sonne, rysing
from the braunches, or bodie of the
same, is gathered and dried at the
sonne, and is so made perfecte cinomome.

nomome. Neare vnto this, is another Iland, called Beda, greater and larger, then anye of the Ilandes of Molucca. In this Iland groweth the
The nut
meg tree
Nutmegge, whose tree is bigge & highe, and much lyke vnto the walnutte tree, for as is the walnutte, so is this fruite defended with a double couering, as fyrste with a grene huske, vnder the whiche is a thinne skinne or rimme like a nette, encompassing the shell of the nutte : which skinne we call the flowre of the nutmegge, but of the Spanyardes, it
Mace.
is called mace, an excellent and hole some spyce. The other couering, is the shell of the nutte, within the
The nut
megge
Ginger
which is the fruite it selfe, which we call ẙ nutmegge. Ginger groweth here and there in all the Ilandes of this Archipelagus, or mayne sea. Of the whiche, some is sowen, and some groweth of it selfe. But that which is sowen, is the better. The herbe
of

of this, is lyke vnto that which beareth saffrane, and hath hys roote,
(which is Ginger,) much lyke vnto
the same. In this meane time came
two other shyppes out of Spayne:
whereof the one sayled directely to
the poynte of Aphrica, called Promontoriū Promontorium
bone spei: And the other by the greate
mayne South sea, to the coastes of bone spei
that continent oz fyrme land wher-
of we haue spoken here beefoze. It
shall suffyse that we haue hetherto
declared of the nauigacions whiche
the Spanyardes attempted by the
Weste to sayle into the Easte, by the
strayghte of Magellanus, where the
passage by Sea is open into the
Easte, by the continente oz fyrme
lande of the newe wozlde, called
America. Nowe therefoze lette vs Colūbus
retourne to the other Nauigaci- the admi-
ons of Columbus, otherwyse called ral, fyrst
finder of
the Admyzall, who longe beefoze the newe
                    K.li.   was Ilandes

was the fyrst fynder of the newe Islandes, and of the sayde mayne or fyrme land, and yet founde not that strayght or narow sea, by the which Magellanus sayled from the West into the East.

¶ The thyrde nauigation of Christophorus Columbus.

IN the yeare of Christ. 1498. Columbus the Admiral departed from Spayne with eyght foistes, and arryued fyrst at the Ilandes of Medera, where he deuyded hys nauie into two partes. For. v. of these shippes he directed to the Iland of Hispana: & with the residue, he sailed towarde the south, entendinge to passe ouer the Æquinoctial line, and from thense to turne towarde the West, to searche suche landes as were hetherto vnknowen to the Christian men. Coming therfore to Caput ueride, he sailed to the burninge line, called Torrida zona where he found so great heate, that he

the Ilandes of Medera

Hispana, or Hispaniola.

Greate heate vnder the burning lyne.

he was in daunger of death: but re=
turninge his shyppes towarde the
West, he found a moze holsome ayze
and (as God woulde) came at the
length to a lande well inhabyted,
where there came agaynst hym and
his, a bote with. xxiiij. young men,
armed with bowes, arrowes, and
shieldes, couering only theyz pziuie
membzes with a clothe of Gossam=
pine cotton, hauing also very longe
heare. The admirall, (as well as he
could by signes) allured them to cō=
municacion . But they trusted not
our men, fearing some deceate. The
Admirall perceauing that he could
nought pzeuayle, by signes and to=
kens, he determined with Musical
instrumentes to appeale their wild=
nesse. As the minstrelles therefoze
blewe theyz shaulmes, the barba=
rous people dzew neare, suspecting
that noyse to bee a token of warre,
whereupon they made ready theyz

Signes ✚
pointing

bowes and arrowes. But the Spa
niardes drawinge nearer vnto thē,
caste certayne apparell into theyr
bote, willing by this token of frendshippe to concile them, although all
were in vayne. For they fled all a-
waye. Wherefore the Admyrall departing frō thence, came to a region
called Parias, wel inhabited & ful of ciuile people, declaring muche huma-
nitie toward straūgers. They shewed our men Pearles and Gold, &
such other riches, desyring them to
come a land, where they gētelly entreated them. When our mē asked
them where they had suche plentie
of golde: they (with home poynting
was in the stede of speach) declared
by signes and tokens, that thei had
it in certayne mountaines, and that
thei could not without great daunger resort thether, by reason of certaine fearse beastes in those partes,
and also because of the cruell people
called

called Canibales, whiche inhabite those
mountaynes. But the Admiral, be=
cause his wheate fayled, was enfor=
sed to departe thence. Dyrectinge
therfore his viage toward ẏ North
easte, he came to the Iland of Hispana,
where he found all thinges consou=
ded and out of ordre. For the Spa=
nyardes which were lefte in the I=
landes, refused to obeye the Admi=
rall and his brother, mouinge gre=
uous cōplayntes agaynste them be=
fore the king of Spaine, and at the
length sente them thether bound.

⸿ Howe Petrus Alonsus soughte
    newe Ilandes.

After that the Admyrall hadde
  incurred the indignacion of
the Kynge, manye of hys compani=
ons, suche as hadde been broughte
vppe with him, and were experte
Sea menne, decreede to searche
other partes of the worlde yet vn=
          K, iiij.   knowen,

vnknowen. Among which number was *Petrus Alonsus*, who with a shippe wel furnished, sayled to *Parias*, & from thence to *Curtana*, where he begon to exercyse marchaundise with the inhabitantes, receauinge Pearles for belles and nedles. Entring also into the land, he was honourably entertayned. In their woodes, he saw innumerable Peacockes, nothinge vnlyke vnto oures, sauing that the males differ litle from the females. In this region are great plentie of Phesantes. *Alonsus* departinge from hense, sailed to the regiō of *Canchietes*, beyng sixe dayes sayling frō *Curtana*, toward the West. In this region is great abundaunce of golde, Popingiayes, Gossampine cotton, & moste temperate ayre. From hence he sayled into another fruiteful regiō, but inhabited with wilde menne, which could by no gentilnes be allured to frendshippe. Departinge therefore from

Parias.

Curtana.

Pearles for belles & nedles

Peacockes.

Phesāts

The Region of Cāchietes

from thence, he came to the region
of Ciniana, whereas pearles are found
in great plentie: but before he came
there, he chaunced to come amonge
the Canibales: agaynst whom, dischar-
geing a piece of ordinaūce, he droue
thē easely to flight. But Alonsus thus
laden with pearles, returned home
into Spayne.

The re-
gion of
Ciniana.

Pearles

¶Howe Pinzonus, companion to
the Admirall, sought newe I-
landes.

Vincētius, otherwise called Pinzonus
in the yeare of Christe. 1499.
prepared foure brigantines, & sailed
fyrst to the Ilandes of Canaria, & from
thence to Caput ueride. Frō whence directing his biage toward the south
farre beyonde the Equinoctial lyne, he
found men in a certayne Iland, but
such as he could by no meanes con-
cyle vnto him. Therefore leauinge
them, he came to another lande, in
whiche were innumerable naked
people

Naked
people.

people, diſſimuling that thei deſired to ioyne frendſhip with the Spaniardes. And whereas one of our mē caſte a bell amonge them oute of the ſhippe, they againe caſt to the Spanyardes a maſſe oʒ piece of golde: which, one of oure companye ſomewhat to bolde, attemptinge to take vp, they ſodeynlye toke him and caried him awaye with meruelous ſwiftenes: but our mē leauing their ſhippes, made haſt to help theyʒ fellowe, in ſo muche that the matter came to handſtrokes. This conſlict was ſo ſharpe, that our men hadde muche a doe to eſcape with theyʒ lyues, by reaſon of the fearſenes of the barbarians. Departing therefoʒe frō thence, they ſayled toward the Noʒtheaſte, and came to the region of Payra, ꝥ ta the Ilandes neare aboute the ſame in the whiche are woodes of ſanders wherewith the marchaūtes lade theyʒ ſhippes, and carie

Gold foʒ belles.

A cōflict betwene the wild men and the Spaniardes.

The Region of Payra.

woodes of Sanders.

carie it into other conntreys. In this Region allo growe the trees, whiche beare Cassia fistula of the belte kynd. There is allo founde a foure foted bealt of móltrous lhape, whole former parte is lyke vnto a wolfe, lauing that the feete are lyke vnto the fete of a man, with eares like an owle: Hauinge allo beneath his comon belye, another belye lyke vnto a purle oʒ bagge, in which he kepeth his yonge whelpes lo longe, vntyll they be able lafely to wäder abʒode alone, and to geat theyʒ meate with oute the he pe of theyʒ parentes. The whelpes while they are verye yong, neuer come out of this bagge but when they lucke. This poʒtentous bealt with her thʒee whelpes, was bʒoughte to Ciu le in .Spaine, and from thence to Granata.

Col

¶ Of the foure nauigacions of *Americus uespucius* to the newe Ilandes.

Americus uespucius, beyng sent with *Christophorus Columbus*, in the yeare of Christ. M.cccc.xcij. at the commaundement of Ferdinando king of Castile, to seke vnknowē landes, and wel instructed in sayling on the sea, after a fewe yeares, set forward sowre viages of hys owne proper charges. That is to witte, two vnder the sayd king Ferdinando, and two other vnder Emanuel, king of Portugale, of the which he himselfe wryteth after this maner.

¶ The fyrste viage of *Americus uespucius*.

IN the yere of christ, M.cccc.xcvij the.xx.daye of Maye, we came with foure shippes, to the fortunate Ilandes, called *Insulæ fortunatæ*, where the North pole hath his eleuacion. xcvij.degrees, &.xl.minutes. And from

Ferdinādo kinge of castile

Insulæ fortunate

frō thence within the space of. xxvij
dayes, we came to a lād moꝛe West=
warde then the foꝛtunate Jlandes,
where the Noꝛth pole was eleuate
xvi. degrees: where also we founde
a nacion of naked people, of innume= Naked
menne.
rable multitude, whiche as sone as
they sawe vs, fled to the next moū=
tayne. Frō hence within two dayes
sayling, we came to a safe poꝛt wher
we founde manye men, which with
much adoe, we could scarcely allure
to communicaciō, although we pꝛo=
fered them belles, lokinge glasses,
cristallyne cuppes, and suche other
iewelles. But at the length perceaↄ Wylde
men allu
red with
gētlenes
uing our good wyll and liberalitie
towarde them, they came to vs by
heapes, and ioyned frendshyp with
vs without all feare. They goe all
as naked as they came foꝛth of their
mothers wombe.   They suffre no
heare on their bodie sauing only on
theyꝛ head, in so much that they pul
of

of ȳ heares of their bꝛowes. They

People, expert tu swimminge.

are all so perfectelye exercysed in swimminge, that they can continue therein, foꝛ the space of two leages without any thinge to beare thē vp and especiallye the women. Theyꝛ weapons are bowes and arrowes. They arme theyꝛ arrowes with ȳ teeth of beastes and fyshes, bycause they lack Irō ⁊ other metals. They kepe warre against their boꝛderers whiche are of straunge language. They fyght not foꝛ the enlargeing of theyꝛ dominion, foꝛasmuche as they haue no Magistrates: noꝛ yet foꝛ thincrease of riches, because thei are contente with their owne commodities: but onely to reuenge the death of theyꝛ pꝛedicessours. At theyꝛ meate, they vse rude and barberous fashions, lying on the groūd

Cadens hanging betwene trees,

without any table clothe, oꝛ couerlet. They slepe in certayne greate nettes made of Gossampine cotton and

and hanged a lofte in the ayre bee-
twene trees. Theyr bodies are verye smothe and clene by reason of
theyr often washinge. They are in
other thinges sylthy and withoute
shame. Thei vse no lawful coniunc-
tion of mariage, but euery one hath
as many women as him listeth, and
leaueth them agayn at his pleasure
The women are very fruiteful, and
refuse no laboure al the whyle they
are with childe. They trauayle in
maner withoute payne, so that the
nexte day they are cherefull and a-
ble to walke. Neyther haue they
theyr bellies wrimpeled, or loose, &
hanginge pappes, by reason of bea-
ringe manye chyldren. Theyr
houses and cabbens, are all in common. Theyr houses are fas-
shyoned lyke vnto belles: and
made of greate trees fastened together, couered wyth the leaues
of

Women
in comē.

Women
very strō-
ge and
fruitful.

Houses
made of
trees.

of date trees, and made very strōge
against wind and tempestes. They

Houses
of maruei-
lous big-
nes.

are also in some places so great, that
in one of them sire hūdreth persons
may lodge. Thei vse euery seuenth
or eyght yeare, to remoue ἢ chaūge
theyr dwelling places, because that
by theyr longe continuaunce in one
place, the ayre shoulde bee infected.
They vse no kynd of marchaundise
or bying and selling, beyng content
onely with that which nature hath

Ryches
ἢ super-
fluities
cōtēned

lefte them . As for Golde, Pearles,
precious stones, iewelles, and suche
other thinges, which we in Europa
esteme as pleasures and delicates,
they sette noughte by . They haue

Bread of
a certain
roote.

no kynde of corne. Theyr common
fedinge, is a certayne roote whiche
they drye and beate ἢ make floure
or meale therof. They eate no kynd

Mans
flesh eatē

of flesse except mans flesse: for they
eate all suche as they kyl in theyr
warres, or oherwise take by chaūce
When

When he had thus vewed the coun=
treye, and cōsydered the maners of
the people, we determyned to saylē
further, downe by the landes syde;
and came after a few daies, to a cer=
tayne hauen, where we sawe about
twentie greate houses, raysed vppē
muche after the faschion of belles:
There came vnto vs a great multi=
tude of mē vnder pretense of frend=
shyp. Some swimminge, and somē
in botes. Who, as sone as thei drew
neare vnto vs, sodeynly bent theyr ⸿ cōſlich
bowes against vs, where we defen=
ded oure selues manfully. In this
bickeringe, we slewe of them about
twentie, beesyde manye that were
wounded: But of our mē, were on=
lye fyue hurte, whiche were all per=
fectelye healed. Thus departingē
from this hauen, we sayled on, and
came to another nacion, in cōuersa=
cion and tongue vtterlye differing
from the fyrst. For comming oure of

L.4.   oure

our shippe, we were very frēdly en-

A gentle nacion

treated of thē, where we continued for the space of nyne dayes . This

Parias

region is very fayre, and fruitefull, hauinge manye pleasaunt woodes, which continue grene all the yeare

Fruites vnlike vnto oures.

longe . They haue fruites innume- rable, vtterlye vnlyke vnto oures. The Region is situate dyrectelye vnder the lyne, called Tropicus Canceri. The inhabitantes them selues, call it Parias. Saylinge farre beyond this Region , and ouerpassinge manye

Gold e- uery where.

countreyes and nacions , fyndinge Gold euery where, (but in no great quantitie) we came to another na- cion full of gentlenesse and humani- tie, where we rested. xxvij. dayes. These people made greuous com- playnte vnto vs , that there was,

Canibales

not farre frō them, a certayne fearse and cruell nacion, whiche be red the sore, and made incursion into theyr
countrey

countreye at a certayne tyme of the yeare, kyllinge them and violentlye carying them awaye, to thintent to eate them, in so muche that they were not able to defend them selues agaynste theyr fearseneise. Whiche thinge when they hadde so lamentablye declared vnto vs, and we hadde made them promyse that we woulde reuenge theyr so manye iniuries, they ioyned vnto oure company seuen of theyr men. Thus we wente forward: and after seuen dayes, came to an Ilande, called ^{uy;} where these fearse people dwelte: Who, as sone as they hadde espyed vs, came armed agaynste vs. We ioyned with them in battaile, which contynued for the space of twoo houres. At the length we droue them to flyghte, and slewe and wounded a greate numbre of them,

An expedicion agaynst ŷ Canibales

and

and toke .xxb. captiues. But of our men was onely one slayne, and .xxi. wounded, & shortly after restored to health. We gaue to those seuē mē which went with vs, thre menne of oure prisonners and foure women, whom with greate reioysinge they caried with them into theyr countreye: and we returninge home toward Spaine, with many captiues came fyrste to a porte of Spayne called Calicium, where we solde oure priesoners, and were ioyefullye receaued: In the yeare of Christ. M. cccc.xcix. the.xb. daye of Octobre.

¶The seconde viage of Vesputius.

IN the moneth of May folowing Vespucius attempted another viage and came by the Ilādes of Canaria, euen vnto the burninge lyne, called the Equinoctial lyne. Torrida zona, and founde a lande beeyonde the Equinoctial line, toward the south.

South, where the South pole is
eleuate fyue degrees. And wheras
he coulde fynde no apte enteraunce
into the land, and sayled vp & down
alonge by the same, he espyed a bote
in which was aboute twentie men:
who, as sone as they saw the Spanyardes, lepte into the Sea and e-
scaped all, except two, which they
toke. In theyr bote which they for-
soke, were founde soure young men
which they had by force taken oute
of another countrey, hauinge theyr
priuie members newelye cutte of.
These, *Vesputius* toke into his shippes
and learned by theyr signes and to-
kens, that they hadde been taken of *Canibales.*
the *Canibales* and should shortly haue
been eaten. But departinge from
these costes, & saylinge on forward,
they came to a commodious hauen,
where they founde muche people,
with whom they ioyned frendshyp,
and fell to chaungeinge of ware, re-

ceauing

ceauinge for one bell,fyue hundreth
Pearles.In this lande they drinke
a certayne kynde of wyne , made of
the iuyse of fruites and sedes,being
lyke whyte and redde sydar . Departinge from hence , and saylinge
yet further,they founde a certayne
Ilande in which was a beastly kind
of people,and simple , yet very gen-
tie.In this Ilande is no freshe water: but they gather the dew which
in the night season falleth vpon certayne leaues muche lyke vnto the
eare of an Asse . They lyue for the
moste parte,by sea fishe. They haue
no cotages or houses: but haue certayne broade leaues , wherewith
they defende them selues from the
heate of the Sunne ,but not from
showres:but it is verye lykely,that
it rayneth but lyttle in that Iland.
Vespatius wyth his companye departinge from hence, sayled vnto another Ilande:into the whiche when
he

he hadde entered, he founde certayne cotages, and in them two old
women, and three young wenches,
whiche were of so greate stature,
that they marueyled thereat. And
whereas oure menne stryued with
them to bringe them to the shyppe,
to thintente to haue caryed them
into Spayne, they espyed cominge
toward them syxe and thyrtie men,
yet of muche greater stature then
were the women, bearing with the
bowes, arrowes, and great stakes
lyke vnto clubbes: at the syghte of
whome, oure menne beinge afrayd,
made haste to theyr shyppes. But
these Gyauntes folowinge them
euen to the Sea syde, bended theyr
arrowes towardes the Spanyardes, vntyll they discharged two
pieces of ordinaunces, wyth the
horryble sounde whereof, they
were immediatly driuen to slight.
Oure menne therefore departinge
L.iiii.   from

from thence, called that Ilande, the Ilande of Giauntes. And came to another nacion, which frendlye entreated them, and offered them many Pearles: in so muche that they boughte. xix. markes weyghte of pearles, for a smal price. They gaue vs also certayne shelfysshes, of the whiche some conteyned in them a hundreth and thyrtie Pearles, and some fewer. Departinge frō thence they came to the Ilande of *Antigla*, which *Columbus* had discouered a few yeares before. Leauinge this, they sayled directely to *Calisium*, a porte of Spayne, where they were honourablye receaued.

Pearles

A hundreth & xxx. pearles in one shelfishe.

Antiglia.

Calisium

☞ The thyrde viage of *Vesputius.*

Vesputius beyng called frō Castile to serue Emanuel the King of Portugale, in the yeare of Christe, M.cccc.ii. the tenth daye of May, departed from the haue of lisburne, and

and sayled downe by the coastes of the sea Atlantike, vntil he came vnder the Equinoctial lyne. And the .xvij. daye of Auguste, they arryued at a certayne lande where they found a kind of beastly people. This land is situate toward the South, fyue degrees beyonde the Equinoctial lyne. A greate multitude of the inhabitantes wer gathered together, and as wel as they coulde by signes and poyntinges, desired oure men to come alande & to see theyr countrey. There were two in the shippe, whiche toke vpon thē to vewe the land, & learne what spyces or other commodities might be had therein. They were appoynted to returne within the space of fiue daies at the vttermost. But when eyght dayes were now paste, they whiche remayned in the shippes, heard yet nothing of theyr returne: wheras in the meane time great multitudes of other people of the

the same lande resorted to the Sea
syde, but could by no meanes be allured to communicacion . Yet at
the length they broughte certayne
women, which shewed them selues
familier towarde the Spaniardes:
Wherupon they sent forth a young
man, beyng very strong and quicke,
at whom as the women wondered,
and stode gasinge on him and feling
his apparell: there came sodeynly a
woman downe from a mountayne,
bringing with her secretely a great
stake, with which she gaue him such
a stroke behynde , that he fell dead
on the earth. The other womenne
foorthwith toke him by the legges,
and drewe him to the mountayne,
whyle in the meane tyme the men
of the countreye came foorth with
bowes and arrowes, & shot at oure
men. But the Spaniardes dischar-
geing foure pieces of ordinaunce a-
gaynst them, droue them to flighte.
The women also which had slayne

Fearse &
cruell
women,

the yong man, cut him in pieces eué
in the sight of the Spaniardes, she-
winge them the pieces, and rosting
them at a greate fyre. The mé also
made certayn tokens, wherby they
declared that not past. viij. daies be
fore, they had in lyke maner serued
other christiá mé. Wherfore ý Spaniardes hauinge thus sustayned so
greuous iniuries vnreuenged, departed ȝ euyl wil: sayling therfore
further toward ý south, they foúd a
nació of great multitude, ȝ of much
gételer códicions, with whó thei re-
mained. viij. daies, bartering ȝ chã-
geing ware ȝ thé. Sayling on yet
farther, they wét beyond ý line called *Tropicus Capricorni*, where the south
pole is eleuate. 32. degrees: ȝ wheras in those parts thei foúd no great
riches, they sailed yet further south
ward vntill ý pole was eleuate. liij.
degrees: where thei came into such
a tempeste, that they were enforsed
to gather vppe theyr sayles , and
to

A ciuile
people.

the south
pole ele-
uate. liij
degrees.

to rowe only with the maste, directing theyr viage toward the costes of Ethiopia, from whence they returned againe to Lisburne in Portugale.

Lisburne

℣ The fourth viage of
Vesputius.

THis nauigatiō was attempted in the peare of Christ. M.cccc. lij. but was not brought to the ende hoped for, by reason of a missortune which chaunced in the goulfe of the sea Atlantike. *Vesputius* entended in this viage to sayle to the Ilande of *Melcha*, beyng in the East, in which is sapde to be great ryches, & the station of restinge place of all shippes comming frō the goulfe *Gangeticus*, & from the Indian sea. This *Melcha*, is situate more toward the West, and *Calicut* more encliininge towarde the south. *Vesputius* came fyrst to ye grene Ilādes, called *Insule ucrides:* and sayled from them to *Serraliona*, beynge in the South

the Ilād of melcha

Calicut

Insule ucrides.

Southe partes of Ethiopia : from whence saylinge on yet further, he sawe in the middest of the sea an Iland, high and merueylous : where also the M. Pylate of this nauie, lost his shippe by running vpon a rocke: but all the mariners escaped. This shippe was of thre hundreth tunne, and had in it al the power of the nauie. When *Vespurias* had entered into the Iland, he found it rude and vnhabited: yet was it full of byrdes: but had no beastes except Lisertes with forked tayles, and Serpentes. Thus makinge prouision for necessaries, he was enforced to returne to portugale, failing of his purpose.

A shippe wracke.

Lisertes and Serpentes

¶How the king of Portugale subdued certayn places in India : and of the ryche Cytie of Malacha.

For asmuche as therefore in the yeares folowinge, there were more often nauigacions made from the

the West by the south into the East, and the Portugales had now foūde a safe passage by the sea, they thought it expedient for theyr better safetie, to make certaine fortificacions and places of refuge in the Easte. The which theyr intent the better to accomplishe, king Emanuel appoynted one Alphonsus an experte man on the sea, to be captayne of this viage. Who, desyring to reuenge the losses and iniuries which the Portugales had before sustained, sayled directly to Aurea Chersonesus, now called Malacha, a merueylous great and riche citie, whose king is an infydel of the secte of the Moores: for euen thus farre was the secte of Mahumet extended. Alphonsus therfore at his coming thether besieged the cytie, & made warre agaynst the Saracens whiche helde the same. In this conflict a greate noumber of theyr enemies beynge slayne, the Portugales entered

the Portugales bild fortes in the East partes.

Alphōsus

Aurea chersonesus,

the great & ryche cytie of Malacha

Saracēs

Malacha besieged

tred into the citie by forse, and kept
the same, permitting free libertie to
theyr souldiers to spoyle, kyll, and
burne. The king himselfe, fyghting
bpon an Elephante, and beyng sore
wounded, sledde with the resydue
of his companye. A greate numbre
of the Moores were slaine with the
losse of a fewe Portugales : manye
were taken, and great spoyle caried
awaye, in the whiche were seuen
Elephantes, and all kyndes of ordinaunces perteyning to the warres,
made of copper, to the noumbre of
two thousande pieces. The cytye
beynge thus taken and sacked, and
the enemyes drieuen to flyghte,
Alphonsus the Capitayne the better
to proupde for the sauegarde of the
Christians, buylded a stronge forte
at the mouth or entraunce of the riuer which runneth through ý citie.
At this time, that is to witte, in the
peare

the king
fighteth
on an e-
lephaut.

plēty of
copper.

yeare of Chriſt. M.ccccc.xij. there
were in Malacha many ſtraũgers and

marchauntes of dyuerſe nacions,
whereby the cytie was repleniſhed
with great ryches and abundaunce
of ſpyces. They of theyr owne mo=
cion, deſyred to make a leage with
Alphonſus, and were of him gently re=
ceaued :   So that for theyr better
ſafetie, he permitted them to dwell
in the houſes neare about the forte.
And by this meanes, this markette
towne was reedified and broughte
to muche better ſtate then euer it
was before. Theſe thiges thus hap
pely atchiued, & al thinges in Malacha
ſet in good order, Alphonſus leauing in
the forte a garriſon of .bi. hundreth
valiante ſouldiours , returned into
India, where he beſieged the chieſe
caſtell of the cytie of Goa, which (he) a
fewe yeares beefore, hadde with no
ſmal daunger of our men, and great
ſlaughter of their enemies, ſubdued
vnder

the dominion of Emanuel kynge of Portugale, ꝙ was nowe possessed of the mores, he manfully recouered agayne, and enforsed them to render vp thesame. Also the ambassadours of the kinge of Narsinga, the kinge of Cambaia, and the king of Grosapha with the legates of dyuers other kinges and Princes, offered them selues to be at a leage wyth Alphonsus, ꝙ thereupon broughte theyr presentes vnto hym. No lesse powre and dominion obtayned the king of Spayne in the Ilandes of the Weste partes: In so muche that at his commaundement, were buylded sixe townes in the Ilandes of Cuba   Lykewyse in the Ilande of Iucatana, was buylded a greate cytie wyth fayre houses. The Ilande of Cozumella, the Spanyardes called Sancta Crux, beecause they came fyrste thether

The Ambassadors make a leage wyth Alphósus

the west Ilandes

Cuba.

Iucatana

Cozumella or Sancta Crux.

M.i.   in

in Maye, on the daye of the Inuencion of the Crosse. In the Ilande of Hispana or Hispaniola, were erected. 28. suger presses, to presse ÿ sugre whiche groweth plentifully in certaine canes or redes of the same coūtrey. Frō hence also is brought the wood of Guaiacum, otherwyse called, Lignum sanctum, wherewith dyuerse diseases are healed by the order of the newe dyete.

⛌ Of the Iland of Medera, and the fortunate Ilādes, otherwyse called the Ilandes of Canaria.

BEtwene Spaine & the Ilādes of Canaria, is the Ilande of Medera, which the Spaniardes in our time founde vnhabited and saluage. But perceauinge that the soyle thereof, was very fruitefull, they burnt the woodes, and made the ground apt to bringe foorth corne, and buylded many houses, and so tilled the same, that

that at this day is no where founde
a moze fruiteful lande. It hath in it
many spzinges of fresshe water and
goodly ryuers, vpon the which are
bylded manye sawe mylles, where= Sawe
with manye fayze trees, lyke vnto milles.
Ceder & Cypzesse trees, are sawed ffayze
and cut in sunder, wherof are made tree of
most fayze tables, coberdes, cofers,
and chayzes, and such other curious
wozkes made of wood. These trees
are of redde colour, & swete sauour,
the bodies and bzaunches whereof
are bzoughte into Spayne in great
plentie. The Kynge of Poztugale
thought it good to plante in this I=
land, that kynde of redes in which Suger.
suger groweth:wherin he was not
deceaued in his opinion. For they
growe there moste fruitefully, and
beare suger which excelleth the su=
gre of Candye oz Sicilia. There were
also vynes bzoughte out of Candye vynes.
and planted in this Ilande, where
      M.ii.   they

they prosper so wel, that for ye moste part they bring forth more grapes then leaues, and those very great. In this Iland is also great plentie of Partriches, wyld Doues, & Peacockes, wild bores, & diuers kindes of other beastes, which onely possessed the Iland before men dyd inhabite the same. Also the Ilandes called the Ilandes of Canaria. Insule fortunatæ, (whiche are nowe called Canaria, for the multitude of Dogges which are in them) are sayd to be no lesse fruytefull. These Ilandes are tenne in noumbre, of the which seuē are inhabited, & thre remaine desolate. They which are inhabited, are called by these names: *Fracta lauces, Magna sors, Grancanaria, Teneriffa Ginera, Palma,* and *Ferrum.* At Columbus first comming thether, the inhabitantes went naked, without shame. religiō or knowledge of God But in successe of time, foure of the greatest I-
Christiās lādes embraced the Christian faith.

They

They haue eche of them a priuate language. Teneriffa and Crancanaria, are bigger then the other. Teneriffa maye be sene afarre of, to the distaunce of fiftie leages, in a fayre & clere daye. The reason whereof is, that in the middest of the Iland, ryseth a maruelous great & strong rock, which is thought to be .xb. leages high, & casteth foorth continuallye greate flames of fyre & pieces of brimstone, as doth the monnt Etna in the Iland of Sicilia. The people of these Ilades, lyue with barlye bread, flesshe, and mylke. They haue also greate plentie of Goates, wylde Asses, and Fygges. They lacke wyne and wheate.

A mont of burninge & brimstone.

Fygges

¶ Whether vnder the Æquinoctial circle or burninge lyne (called Torrida zona) be habitable Regions.

Libr. i.
Capit. b.

Pius secundus (otherwise called Eneas Siluius,) of this question, wryteth in this maner. It hath been muche doubted whether habitable regiōs maye be founde vnder the Equinoctial lyne. Eratosthenes is of thoppinion, that the ayre is there verye temperate, So thinketh Polybius also, affirming that the earth is there verye highe, and watered with many showres, Possidonius supposed that there is no Mountaynes vnder the Equinoctial. Some thoughte that the Equinoctial lyne was exteded beyond the earth ouer the mayne Ocean sea: whiche thinge the Poet Homere semeth to insinuate, where he faineth that the horses which drawe the chariote of sunne, drinke of the Ocean sea, and the sunne it selfe to take his norishe-ment

Eratosthenes.

Polybius.

Possido-nius.

the Equinoctial line

the poet Homere

ment of the same. Whiche sentence Macrobius, also foloweth. Neither was Albertus Magnus farre from this opinió, who supposeth ý the sunne draweth vp so much moysture vnder the Equinoctial circle, as engendreth the cloudes vnder the poles, where by reason of thexcedinge coldnesse, ayre is continualli turned into water. But Ptolomeus thinketh the earth to bee extended beyonde the Equinoctial, whereas he placeth a part of the Iland of Taprobana, vnder the Equinoctial, & also many nacions of the Ethiopians. Many haue thought that thearthly Paradyse was sette vnder that lyne : which opinion is contrary to thauctoritie of holy scripture which witnesseth the two famous fluddes Tigris and Euphrates to springe oute of Paradise : whiche neuerthelesse we know from the North partes to fal into the goulfe called sinus Persicus: but as concerninge the heate vnder the

Side notes:
Macrobius.
Albertus Magnus.
Ptolomeus.
Taprobana
Ethiopes
Tigris & Euphrates.
sinus Persicus.

Equinoctial lyne, the nearenesse of the sunne, or the directe beames of the same, are no sufficiente causes why vnder that line should be no habitable regions, if we consider how those places are otherwyse shadowed, & tempered with the moystenes and dewes of the nightes, which are all the yeare throughe of equal length with the dayes. Yet wyl no man denye, but that vnder the Equinoctial throughoute all the burninge lyne there are manye wildernesses and desolate places, lacking water, and incommodious for the lyfe of man: Albeit euen in Ethiopia, people dwell neare to the ryuers and woodes. Plinie also sayth that one Dalion, and and Aristocleon, and Bion, and Basilides, went Southward beyonde Meroe whiche is almoste vnder the Equinoctial. And that Simonides who writte the descrip
ction

cion of Ethiopia, dwelte fyue yeres in Meroe: whiche Jlande (beeynge in the fyrme lande and compassed aboute wyth the Ryuer of Nilus) he affyrmed to bee situate. 972. thousande pases beeyonde Syenes of Egypte, as the searchers of Nero declared. But at Sienes the Astronomers appoynte the sommer conuersion of the sunne: and that there the burning lyne beginneth, beinge distaunte from the Æquinoctial foure and twentie degrees, that is, twelue thousande furlonges. Wherby we maye perceaue that Meroe is situate some what beeyonde the myddest betwene the Equinoctial and Sienes. Ptolomeus also descrybeth the Region of Agisimba to bee inhabited beeyonde the Equinoctial.

Lykewyse the Mountaynes of the Mone, called Montes Luna

out

the Jlãd of Meroe

Syenes in Egipte.

The conuersiõ of the ssue.

Of the furlõges of Italie viij. dos make one Italiẽ mple, cõtepning 8.m, pases.

Agisimba

Montes Lane.

of the which, the fennes oz marifes
of the riuer Nilus haue their fpzing &
oziginall. He addeth hereunto that
there are certayne Ethiopians called Anthropophagi, that is, fuch as eate
mans flefhe, which inhabite regiõs
beyond the Equinoctial about the fpace
of.xvi.degrees. And thus the in-
habitacion of men is found to be ex-
tended.x.hundzeth thoufand pafes
beyonde the Equinoctial lyne. Whiche
fpace conteyneth no leffe then two
clymes of the earth. And a clyme is
a pozcion of the wozlde betwene
South and Nozth, wherein
is variacion in length of
of the daye, the fpace
of halfe an houre.

Finis.

¶ Thus endeth the fyfth boke
of Sebastian Munster, of the landes
of Asia the greater, and of the
newe founde landes, and
Ilandes.

1553.

¶ Imprinted at London, in Lom-
barde strete, By Edward
Sutton.

¶ To al aduenturers, and suche as
take in hande great enterprises,

Who hath not of sowrenes felte the bitter taft,
Is not worthy of swetenes to take his repaft.
To cracke the nutte, he must take the payne,
The which would eate the carnell fayne.
Who that of bees feareth the ftinge,
Shal neuer by hony haue great wonninge.
As the swete Rose bringeth forth the thorne,
So is man truely to ioye and payne borne.
The byrde vpon hope byldeth her nefte,
Where oftentymes she hath but euyll refte.
Yet is she not therby dryuen to such feare,
But yᵗ she performeth the same the nexte yeare.
much caftīg of periles doth noble corags swage
Yet do not I commende rafhenes or outrage.
What foles do fable, take thou no hede at all,
For what they know not, they cal phātaftical.
Nought venter nonght haue, is a faying of old
Better it is to blow the cole, then to fyt a cold.
Fortus fortuna adiuuat, the Latin prouerbe faith,
But fayleth to such as faynt and lacke fayth.
God giueth al thinges, but not yᵉ bul by yᵉ horne
The plowmā by trauaile encreafeth his corne.
As fortune faueceth yᵗ mayft be riche or poore,
As Crefus or Irus that beggeth at the dore.

¶ Omnis iacta fit alea.